Maidens, Mothers, Martyrs, & Magic

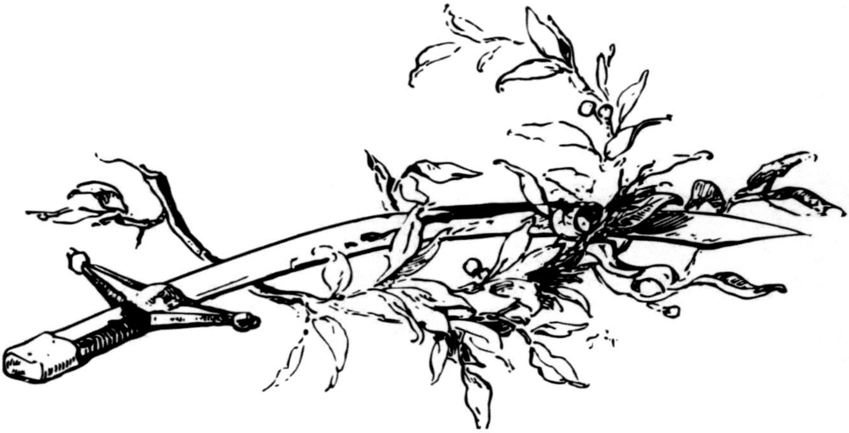

For those who are laying down their weapons and taking off their armor.
For those who are unraveling generational grief while weaving generational joy.
For those disrupting patterns of abuse and embracing compassion and vulnerability.
For those trying to mend their mother wounds.

For my nana, who always believed in my power.

&

For my mother, whose wounded heart gave me a home between its stitches.

Foreword

I used to play in the back of my mother's walk-in closet, creating stories on paper or with my Barbie dolls in the little nook I made behind my mother's clothes. Those were the only moments I felt safe around any part of her. My mother has always been brave, resourceful, highly intelligent, and tenacious. I have her to thank for my grit and my love of literature and writing, but I also have her to thank for my love of escapism. My mother has always been very angry and I've spent a lot of my life hiding from her ire. In hindsight I realize that she was angry because she felt powerless being a young, queer, Black woman at the mercy of a racist, patriarchal, and heteronormative society. Neither of us were ever safe. Life made my mother a warrior, and her mother before her, and her mother before her. And I feel all of their fights and fury coursing through my veins.
When I think of mothers I think of thorny women, I think of open wounds, I think of warriors learning to be gentle. The following poems tell a transgenerational story of maidens, mothers, martyrs, and magic that encapsulates the heartbreak of being a daughter and healing of becoming a mother.

Semi-Sweet

When I was younger, my mother and I
loved to make brownies.
She put all her tenderness into her baking.
If I savored each bite I could taste her love
baked somewhere
between the sugar and chocolate.
We both love chocolate.
Semi-sweet
morsels we mixed into thick batter.

Sometimes when she was irritated with me
she'd make me mix the batter by hand.

Deny me ease.

Make me put elbow grease
into each turn around the mixing bowl
My arms would burn for the semi-
sweetness of her favor.
I'd mix until her frown smoothed
And our conversation was free of clumps.
Until talking to her was as easy as pouring
batter into a baking pan.

Each smile from her was a rogue chocolate chip that hopped away like a
Chocolate frog.
I'd eat them even if they fell on the floor.

Baking with my mother was a memory walk
My mother's mixing bowl a pensieve
in which she opened her mind to me and
Let me find her story between batter and bitterness.
See where sharp edged eggshells mixed into her mannerisms.
See where her love for baking began

and why she put more sweetness into her desserts than she put into her daughter.

My mother and I both relish
in a warm brownie with a scoop of vanilla ice cream on top.
And it's the sameness—the moments where we mix
that reminds me we are part of each other's creation.

Sometimes I wonder what ingredient I am in her recipe.
The flour that forms the foundation?
The cocoa powder that adds depth? The sugar that sweetens her days?
The egg that binds her?

I hope I'm more like the chocolate chips.
Semi-sweet, essential,
wanted enough to chase
if I go rogue.
Dessert enough to love.

Maiden, Mother, Martyr, and Magic

Once upon a time
there was a maiden with stars in her eyes
and a rock in her chest.
She liked to play in the back
of her mother's closet
imagining worlds beyond hers
full of dragons, fairies,
and magic

She imagined she was a witch.
She wondered what magic felt like.
Where boogers came from,
and what would happened
to all of her boogers
when she dies?

Would they glow in the dark or remain
forever unseen like she is in life?
She wondered if boogers
were all she'd leave behind.

Once upon a time there was a maiden
with stars in her eyes,
a rock in her chest,
and a lock in her throat where her voice
should be.
Her imagination was the only loud thing
about her

Her mother was a warrior—
a sword
always unsheathed
Slaying her daughter as she tried to shield
her
Lessons delivered like lacerations
What didn't mark the skin
bruised the mind.

The girl spent her life impaled on the
pointy end.

Knife in the Mattress

My mama told me that her earliest memory was of jumping on the bed.
Unburdened by stress.
That my nana kept a blade beneath the mattress.
That my nana stabbed my papa 23 times
With my mom as witness.

My mama told me that we come from women forged in fire.
that her mother spoke words that cut.
I remember my mother telling me she hated me once...
Some of her words still twist in my gut.
I often wondered how I could be her daughter.
How does a knife give birth to a pillow?
How does the pillow keep from getting sliced open?

I come from warrior women
who never had soft, safe places to repose.
I come from cuss outs, beatings, stabbings
and bitches who will break your nose.

We come from meeting others' needs
to the detriment of our own,
defending our violated boundaries,
turning battlefields into homes.

I come from women whose fear
sharpened them into swords.
Who mistook silence for a shield
leaving their daughters to find truths
 in their unspoken words.

Grief has permeated my maternal line
from as far back as I could find.
Stab wounds that permeate wombs.
Unsmiling photographs with my great-
grandmothers shoulders
hunched over.
Exhaustion and sadness weigh on her
 like armor

Silent killers preserved in sepia.

Satisfaction sacrificed
for survival.

I come from women with short timelines .
Who made more plans for death
than they ever did
for life.

My great-grandmother passed at 54.

My Nana
surrendered to her hospice bed at only 69.
About three times the number
She slashed my papa with her knife.

And I wonder
if my Nana felt alone
I wonder if she felt unheard.
I wonder if it was her last resort
or her first.

I wonder if she knew
that her baby girl was watching.

When my mother smiles,
I still see the razors in her teeth.
She tells me she loves me
with bleeding tongue
and when I hug her
it is metallic and sweet.

She relinquishes her blades to me
because I am not a pillow.

I am a sheathe.

Tired

I've only seen one photo of my great-grandmother. She looked like she didn't even want to be there for it. Her eyes were sunken, her lips turned down,
her shoulders slack, her whole frame
a frown.

She looked
so tired.

She looked so
so tired

She got her final rest at only 54.

I think my mother looks just like her.

Purses

My nana always said
I was born for greatness.

She also said I have terrible taste
in purses.
So she'd always buy me bags.

My nana was the first person
To show me ease–
to show me what it meant
to treat yourself. Nana
liked to eat good, liked
her steak and potatoes
with a Pepsi and a cigarette.

She always kept a Pepsi and some
cigarettes in her purse.
Tucked away next to her receipts and her
grit.

My nana was a lowkey kind of fly.
She had good taste
She had a small collection of Coach and
Michael Kors
But was often donned in Walmart Chique
or Amazon Warehouse couture.
Until she kept blacking out on the
warehouse floor.

Nothing in her purse could help her
anymore.

Nana worked her whole life-until her body
gave her no choice
but to rest.
Nana didn't receive
a lot of tenderness never got to tend to
herself.
For she was a first daughter
And first daughters have to harden.
Stiff leather
So we can carry the family's burdens

My nana didn't finish highschool
capitalism called her from the
classroom to the workforce, said
diplomas and degrees don't
feed families when empty
plates and past due dates were
coming up faster than she could graduate.

My nana came up in a time
where her physical labor
was deemed more valuable
than the thoughts in her mind,
but that didn't stop her from carrying
dreams in her purse
and it didn't stop her from putting dreams
in mine.

My nana carried her family
Right next to her Pepsi, her cigarettes,
her receipts and her grit.
Put little sisters on her shoulders.
Nurtured her nephew's spirits.

My nana always told me
To pack a pen in my purse.
So I could take note of things that inspire me.
She also said whenever I come over
 to bring her a cold Pepsi.

My nana loved offerings
Her love language was gifts
And I realized
my nana was simply asking for
a taste of tenderness.

When she resigned to her hospice bed
she had no purse to hold her things.
She carried nothing but a resolve to pass
peacefully.

My nana always told me
I was born for greatness.
And now she'd say
I have wonderful taste in purses
because I've inherited all of hers
and everyday I pack my courage next to
my water bottle, and my pre-roll.
and I carry ease to all the places
she knew I'd go.

Balloon in a Knife Shop

I envy people who have friendships with their mothers; who have generational camaraderie instead of trauma. I want to feel at ease around my mother but sometimes I can't help but to feel like a balloon in a knife shop when she's around.

Mirror Mirror

My mother
saw me wield my beauty
and felt betrayed
so she sent me into the wilderness with huntsman
Hoping that I would be tamed.
Hoping to deter my audacity
with shame.

I wonder if she knew how many times
I'd be maimed.

Ruby daggers in my diaphragm
many have tried to steal my breath
many have cut and stabbed my flesh
fracturing my vision of who I was.

Never a princess
more like a problem.
A blossom to be nipped in the bud.

Sentenced to death
because my mother feared
I mirror mirrored her too much.

I traversed treacherous trees
forced to fight or fall to my knees.

My journey has been wrought
with danger
and for so long I wandered
wondering how I became an outcast
running from shadows and bloodthirsty
hunters.

I saw my haunted face mirrored
in the knots on menacing trees
Intrusive thoughts constantly
clawed at me
until I stumbled upon a clearing and
found clarity.

I built a cottage and let my feelings live
freely.

Instead of dwarfing myself
I made space for all of me
and I learned that I was never meant
to simply be a queen
but that I was born to be everything.

I became a hermit Happy to garden
even when I got a little Sneezy,
I allowed myself rest when I got Grumpy or
Sleepy,
I gave myself grace when I acted a little
Dopey,

I turned Bashful into bombastic now this
homicidal forest
is looking more hopey.

I became a Doc— a healer
no princess nor queen,
I stroll the forest singing songs to birds
with clipped wings.

And when my mother ventures a visit
disguised as a hag with poison apples,
I greet her with forgiveness
and free her from the cage
of her dark castle.

I invite her to show herself,
to come undone,
to let the wild woman awaken and be
untamed
We don't need the kisses
of kings and princes,
we just need to release our shame.

We charm the forest to our favor,
we smoke trees with our titties out
We no longer live in whispers
but thrive in joyful shouts.
We determine where our beauty lies
No longer needing mirrors to see
eye to eye.

No longer hunted
because we dared to fly.

Apologies

What no one ever tells you about
motherhood is that once you give birth you
are thrust
backwards in your timeline.
Things that you think have healed suddenly
tear open again and you are forced to face
them otherwise you bleed all over your
new baby.
A battle rages within me.
One between maiden and mother.
Connection and ego.
Hurt child and healed woman.

That's why I always come wielding
apologies.

Explanations

Mommy's sorry for yelling at you.
I was overwhelmed and didn't handle it well.
You didn't deserve that.
You deserve space to be who you are

Growing up there was no space for me to be who I am.
So I made space in the back of the closet stole moments of magic
Got lost in my narrations like Narnia

Until I got called back to my campaign

then I'd vacuum-seal my vibrance
Stow away my spirit like out of season sweaters
Abandon my authenticity for armor.

Because home was like the barracks.
Infantry since infancy
Baby, your momma was bred for war

Every mistake I made fanned flames of friendly fire—
a stab in the back.

I have been wounded my whole life.
And I'm trying so hard not to bleed on you.

I have been wounded my whole life
But I promise I will heal for you.

I will unpack my vibrance from the closet,
transform these barracks into a ballroom and
trade my armor for a tutu.

I will wear vulnerability like a pair of dancing shoes.

We don't have to hide.
We don't have to shrink.

In this big beautiful ballroom there is space
For all of you and all of me.

Dance with my Daughter

I make it a point to dance with my daughter
to smile at her—
To show her every gap in my teeth.
She has a gap just like me
A touch of mischief in her grin as we twirl
Like the swirly scribbles she leaves
On the wall—
The ones I won't clean because I refuse to erase
any impressions of her.

I want them to be seen as much as I want her to be heard.

I make it a point to dance with my daughter.
To cradle her
in my arms as we waltz across the floor.
to take her smallness into me and breathe.
to inhale the innocent scent of her hair.
to brush my cheek against her soft ear.
to make her smile with her mischievous teeth.

She slides from my arms and frolics on her
little feet.
She balances
     on
       one
         leg
Spins in a circle
Whips her head.

Audacity in a diaper.

I make it a point to dance with my daughter
Because I wish my mother danced with me.

She taught me to stand aside or
stand and fight
but couldn't show me the delight
of being light
on my feet
because her footsteps were heavy
With shame.

More dictator than dancer
Her joy was pressed to the ground
She only saw mistakes in my grin
So I stumbled to the beat of beat-downs
She balanced on one leg
she stomped...stomped...
stomped me into the ground.

Making me a wallflower
with her coercive choreography.

So I dance with my daughter so I can heal and release.

I dance with my daughter so we both can be free.

Haikus of Her

Bleeding heart of steel
Sharp tongue to pierce your ego.
My mother knows strength

Mothering herself
Since she was a teenager
Raised herself and me.

A mighty soldier
Fighting monsters in her path
Keeping us both whole

Instinct to protect
She shielded me with prayer
Loved me through her food.

Fed my dreams with books
Introduced me to magic
My mother believes.

She has grown softer
My kids call her Halmoni
I love her smile.

Maiden, Mother, Martyr, & Magic: Part Two

Once upon a time,
there was a maiden
impaled on her mother's swords.

The stars in her eyes a guiding light.
The rock in her chest between her and death.

The maiden was a martyr
who became a mother
Who refused to let her children be impaled too.

So one by one
she faced down her wounds—
Pulled at each pike
and transmuted them into poetry.

She picked the lock on her throat with a pen.

and wielded her voice
to wail, to roar, to speak life
where there was once living death.

To tell the rock in her heart it's finally safe to soften.
And to serenade the stars so they're no longer trapped in her eyes
but spread out like the cosmos
sparkling in her children's smiles.

She became a warrior—
empathy unsheathed

Lessons like long hugs.

She learns that magic feels like baby hair
That boss boogers come from toddler noses
That boogers do glow in the dark
When the person they came from is full of light.
And that she no longer has to hide in closets
to feel at home.

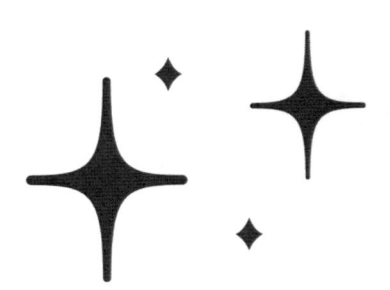

Home Security

I'm insecure about my home.

That's why every picture must be in the most pleasing composition $-90°$ angles. perfectly parallel
So that the smiles on my family's faces don't tip too far downward.

Make sure the plants stay green, silky, and perky
Learn how they like the light
Learn how they take their water
Because just like my children:
They deserve the best—deserve to grow unscathed.

That's why I must be poised in my most pleasing composition
Purposeful
Perfectly parallel
So that the smile on my face doesn't tip too far downward betraying the fact that…

I'm insecure about my home
I grew up with no smiles on the wall..
No green, silky, perky plants
To reach out and say
"You will thrive here".

Morning Miracles

Soft light filters through the curtains as the first rays peak over the mountains bathing them in early morning gold and bathing me in early morning heat. The sky brightens as fast as the seconds tick by, finally revealing the white-blue of early morning from beneath the mystery grey-purple of twilight. I lay on the cool, crisp sheets splayed out on my side of the bed—at least for the moment. The bed is soft, not as soft as the contours of your face as you sleep soundly, mouth gently slack, arms full with two babies whose little hands rest lightly around your middle. I place my hand on each of your chests one at a time, feeling them rise and fall, appreciating the warmth beneath all of your skin. I place my hand on my own chest and breathe in deep and allow the oxygen to fill my capillaries. The air is mixed with lavender and pee. This feels like home. This feels safe. I feel safe. The robins greet us with a high note, your deep yawns are the bass, and our babies' coos are the ambient ad libs that bring it all together. I add my own voice to the melody by singing a thanks to the heavens.

An Imperfect Place

My home is an imperfect place
Where messiness is not a
Failing
but rather
an extension of grace.
A knowing that we are safe.
An acknowledgement that
our world still spins despite its
Many many spills.

Scribbles adorn the walls…
right beneath our family pictures
marks from the little hands
that sprouted from me
making our home more colorful with
their artistic sensibilities.

Beds stripped of soiled
sheets,
cleansed of nightmares, and
imbued with soft soothes.
Laid bare in the knowing
that a happy morning yellow sun
will warm its yellowed threads again.
And that accidents are part of learning
and they are never the end.

Clothes scattered everywhere.
Hanging off the bed and
piled in that special chair.
A sign of indecision.
A sign of excitement.
A sign of our freedom to change and
choose.

There's still blue tape in the bathroom
and so many unfinished projects
Evidence of love's dedication

But also love's need for rest.

Because love is trying its best
to make a masterpiece out of brokenness
like my daughter makes masterpieces from
her broken crayons
because nothing
is ever truly broken–

Only multiplied
so that we can make more beauty,

more freedom,
more   space.

Because there is space.

Space for *joy*

Space for *toys*

Space for *my children*

And *inner child*

to play, to laugh, to run
with open arms. Open minds.
My home has
So many open chambers.
Because my home is a heart.

My home is a magic hearth
where woes warm into smiles.
Where yells soften into whispers.
Where tears turn into laughter
and laughter turns into butterflies
and four spritely spirits turn into one.
Like colors coalescing into a rainbow
Like auras dancing
Like light singing
And as I reach my hands out to thank God,
I feel Love

breathing.

Burp Rag

I was thinking about my life and childhood and started to cry in the living room so I went to my bedroom to hide. I searched for something to wipe my face with and all I could find was my baby's burp rag. It was soft and I thought I should wipe my tears with these all the time. It's comforting.

Motherhood is a portal through which you can never go back only forward. There is no returning, no starting over, no redo, no fast forward. There is only a series of nows and what you do with them. As a mother my greatest hope for my children is that they experience life with no shame and don't allow fear to keep them from living. I hope that they spread goodness wherever they go and that they keep an open heart, open mind, and a wild spirit.

Afterword

Generations of warriors rage within me, but I declare our fight over. I make a brand new bed. I fluff feather down pillows for my foremothers and bestow flower crowns and kisses upon their heads. I lay generational suffering to rest and invite peace to the repast.

I am a gentle warrior.
I sheathe lethal edges
so that softness can thrive at last.

Kaliah the Light is a poet, visual artist, storyteller, mother, and dance enthusiast based in Las Vegas, Nevada. Her work primarily concerns themes of motherhood, bodily autonomy, Black womanhood, and self-love.

As a member of the Spotlight Poetry collective and Reigning Monarchs slam team, Kaliah's work has entranced, electrified, and soothed audiences from the west to the east coast. Kaliah has competed in local, regional, and international poetry slams from Las Vegas to Albuquerque to Baltimore. She is a 2024 Chicharra Poetry Slam Festival Finalist, one of the top 80 poets in the 2024 Womxn of the World Poetry Slam, and the 2024 Utah Arts Fest Underground poetry slam champion.

Kaliah's poetry is influenced by her belief that one must "shadow-work so they can shine". She integrates motifs of light and dark with bold declarations of sovereignty and sensuality as well as joyful descriptions of the safety and softness she's found in motherhood and healing generational trauma. Her goal is to share her fire in hopes of helping others feel empowered, safe, and sacred.

You can find Kaliah the Light on Instagram at @KaliahtheLight.

Made in the USA
Middletown, DE
06 December 2024